the **D**

I

R

T

Dear Heartbroken,

If your heart feels like it's been put through a paper shredder and then stomped on, then you've come to the right place. If you feel like you've been beaten up, used, and tossed away like yesterday's garbage, then this book is for you. If you gave someone your heart only to have them spit on it and turn and run away, then read on. Your heart is aching, throbbing even, and you're crying out for answers but getting nothing but static. You aren't alone. Around the world hearts like yours are melting and tearing, ripping and breaking. The agony of a love gone wrong. The pain of a heart that feels like it will never mend. You are at the end of your rope and you need relief. Fear not, faithful friend, the end is in sight and your heart will hear singing again.

Do you realize that there are only 3 groups of people that have *never* felt like you do right now?

1 **Boring people**—those who have never opened their heart to love.

2 **Crazy people**—those who love but turn off their emotions so they don't have to feel the pain.

3 **Liars**—those who are lying to themselves and to you.

For the rest of us, love and loss are a part of life. So you're not alone. It's going to hurt, and that's okay. Let it hurt. That's why it's called breaking up instead of joy-o-rama. But keep reading and we will get through this.

What's Inside

the dirt

6 come on in ⇢ Dumped? Or dumpee? Either way, you need this book!

8 truth time ⇢ Truth is, breaking up sucks. Question is, what can you do about it?

for the heartbroken

12 it happens ⇢ Breakups will happen and breakups will hurt.

14 see it coming ⇢ Learn these 8 signs the end is near.

16 brace yourself ⇢ Prep for when you have a feeling things are over.

18 the breakup ⇢ What to do (and not to do) when it happens to you.

23 why? ⇢ 10 reasons they might give for breaking up with you.

27 "let's just be friends" ⇢ Why you should beware the affectionate breakup.

29 recovery time ⇢ Take action to get your life back on track!

32 breakup quiz ⇢ How well are you handling the breakup? Take our quiz to find out.

35 trauma treatment ⇢ 3 steps to getting over it.

42 relational rehab ⇢ Tips to guide you from pain to power.

47 breaking the breakup blues ⇢ Control your mind, control your feelings. Making breakups easier to handle.

10 Things **NOT** to do when being dumped. page 20

for the heartbreaker

54 **what do you want?** ••• Get a game plan for what you want, why, and how to break it off.

56 **location, location, location** ••• Don't try this at home.

59 **your choice is reason enough** ••• But here are some others you might identify with.

64 **for girls** ••• Hints for making sure he gets a clue.

66 **guys' turn** ••• The inside scoop on calling it off with your girl.

67 **the clean break** ••• The long and short of how to break away.

72 **say what?** ••• The words you'll need when you're the breaker.

77 **whose fault is it anyway?** ••• Where to lay the blame for your breakup.

80 **breakup prep** ••• Do's and don'ts you need to think about ahead of time.

after it's all over

84 **can we still be friends?** ••• Breaking up questions that need answers.

89 **survivor's manual** ••• The tools you need to make it past the pain.

98 **it's all over** ••• The final word on breakups.

the extras

102 **life support** ••• Scriptural support for your broken heart.

111 **what next?** ••• Prayers and more to help you through.

Dear Heartbreaker,

So you wanna dump someone?

There was a time when you loved them, or maybe you just really thought you loved them. But that time has passed. Now you are frustrated, angry, and just sick of the same ol' routine. The time has come—you know it has—but breaking up is hard to do. You don't want to hurt them. You still care about them—just not like you used to.

Well, this book is for you. Sometimes it's easiest to just walk away. Let them figure it out on their own. But you are a good person. You want to make it easy on them and yourself. You want to exit with style, not selfishness. So now you scream, "How do I do this? How do I live my life the way I want to without destroying the people around me?" Keep reading. This is going to hurt. There will be other things in your life that you will do that will hurt people too, but you still have to do them. You still have to pull the Band-Aid off, even though it hurts.

Truth
Time

Breaking up sucks! There is nothing else to say. But I can't stop there or this would be a really short book. So I will continue. It sucks. Period, the end, and I never want to do it again. I hated it last time and I hated it this time and I will hate it next time. I want to avoid the pain with every fiber of my pain-avoiding being. I want to keep my heart away from Hurtsville. "But how, how, how?" I asked myself. To answer myself I put on my little thinking cap and turned up the juice. "How can I keep from ever having to break up again?" I asked my little thinking-capped self. "Self," I said, "the way I see it, you have 2 options. Either you can swear off dating, thus assuring that you will never have to break up again, or you can promise yourself that you will marry the very next person you date, which will also certainly save you from another gruesome breakup. It's simple, really. Two easy choices for avoiding breakup pain."

Well, I immediately took off that stupid thinking cap. I mean, what kind of ideas were those? (Besides, people were staring and it didn't match my outfit.)

Both options seemed kind of psychotic to me,

'cuz I'm *dang* sure I'm not going to give up the opposite sex. And I'd be an idiot to say, "I swear, the next hottie that comes along and makes me purr is going to be mine! Forever and ever amen!" That ain't happenin'. So now what? If there are only 2 options for avoiding the breakup and I'm not up for either of them, then I guess I only have one solution: get really good at breaking up.

The truth is, my willing participants in this sick little book, that in any dating relationship you have only 2 options: **break up or get married.** That's it. You can't just date for eternity (well, I guess you could, but how lame). And the other nasty little truth that you probably don't want me to mention right now, but what the heck, it's my party, is this: that if you are in high school right now and are reading this book, it's probably because you've figured out the very important but little-accepted fact that we beat to death in our book *Dateable,* and that is that *it will not last.* The relationship that you just broke was not meant to last. It wasn't meant to last because you aren't at a point where it *could* last. You are at a point where the world is your oyster. (I have no idea what that means, but it sounds cool!) The future is yours to grab and ride like a pony at the fair. Okay, a little more exciting than that! But dating was really only a temporary distraction that got you off the track of your real purpose in life. So it's time to get back on track and get through this nightmare called breaking up.

That said, **breaking up still sucks!** I hate it! I hate that you have to go through it. It will be hard no matter which side of the break you are on. But listen, there is hope. This book you hold in your hand, or that you are looking at so rudely over someone's shoulder, will not change the fact that breaking up is one of the worst things you will ever experience. I know, I'm not being Captain Encouragement here, but you will survive this. You will get through the sewer of crappy emotions and break through to the other side. Yeah, there is another side. Just hang in there and we'll get there.

for the

heart

broken

it *happens*

People break up for lots of reasons. Sometimes they are valid, and sometimes they seem flat-out ridiculous. And when you are on the receiving end of the breakage, all reasons will seem stupid. Either way, good reasons or not, you have to face the fact that it's happening. We aren't puppets. Dummies, maybe, but not puppets. We all have free will. That gift allows others to pick and choose who they spend their lives with and when. So breaking up becomes a natural and normal part of life unless you are the one in millions who finds "the one" the first time you ever date. As for the rest of us, breakups will happen, and they will hurt.

Here's a little thought about dating. I know, it's not what you want to hear about, but I promise this is all part of the breaking up stuff. Just humor me. Before you date, it is important to start figuring out what you want in a mate. That's a lot of the deal in dating. But also watch for the stuff you don't want in a mate and move on when it becomes really evident that it ain't happenin' in your current sitch. So think about each crush as training for the ultimate relationship. It's the steps you go through in order to figure out who you are and what you ultimately want, or who you ultimately want, for the rest of your life.

> **Okay, back to our regularly scheduled breakup.**
> Turn the page for some digs on what you can do if you think you are about to be dumped.

Undying trust
in God makes you
wanna say thanks,
even in the middle
of a heartbreak.

see it coming

Yeah, it's a lot easier to think about breaking up with them than for them to break up with you. But here you sit. You can see the crushing blow coming, so what do you do?

Pause. Rewind.
Before we get too deep into this, let's handle one little issue. **A breakup is never an instant decision.** There have been clues along the way. Of course, you may have played blind and chose to ignore them, but they were there. In fact, if you haven't heard the breakup news yet but are wondering if it's coming your way, here are some clues that you are on the path to pain.

8 signs that a breakup is near

Their friends are acting weird. Face it, we always tell our friends what's going on in our love lives, so if his/her friends start to act weird, it might be a clue that something is up.

1

They don't want to talk as much anymore. On the phone they don't seem to want to talk as much as they used to. They cut the convo short or don't seem to want to be on the phone with you.

2

Where's the love? All the nice mushy things they used to say are watered down now. No more cards and cute notes. They aren't saying things like "I love you" or "I miss you" as much anymore. A change in communication might be a sign that a breakup is on their mind.

PDA Alert. Suddenly they won't hold your hand in public. No more arms around you or kisses in the hall. A halt to all public displays of affection is a surefire sign that something is amiss.

Name change. When suddenly you are no longer the boy/girlfriend but are just intro'd as "my friend," you know what's up. In their mind you might have *already* become just a friend.

Fights. If you feel like you just can't seem to do anything without it erupting into major fightage, it's a sign that something is definitely wrong. Whether it's a sign of a breakup or that you're just in an abusive relationship, it's not a good thing.

Caught in the act. If you catch them in a lie about where they were, who they were with, or what they were doing and it isn't 'cuz they were planning your surprise birthday party, then look out. This isn't a good sign for the person's character or the relationship.

You can't do anything right. If it seems like everything you do is wrong or "not how they would do it" or just plain stupid, then they could be letting you know that the end is near.

These are a few signs that don't require telepathic abilities. Just watch, observe, and notice what is happening in the relationship.

Brace Yourself

Now, you may already know the breakup is coming or suspect it based on the list on the last page. **So what can you do?** If you have some advance notice, you are in a great place—well, as great a place as you can be at right now. At least if you see it coming, you can do some advance prep.

First of all, start getting this ancient truth into your head. In his letter to the Ephesians, the apostle Paul says, "For our struggle is not against flesh and blood, but against the rulers, against the authorities, against the powers of this dark world and against the spiritual forces of evil in the heavenly realms" (chapter 6, verse 12 NIV).

This is the thing you will have to remind yourself of over and over and over: This whole deal has very little to do with you and your crush, but it has everything to do with your spirit, your mind, and your thoughts. You aren't battling your crush, you're battling the sinful thoughts you might have that are inconsistent with Scripture. Keep that in your head.

And now **ask yourself a couple of questions**. Well, don't just ask, answer them. These Q's will help you get your mind focused before D-day (Dump Day).

1. Can the pain kill you?
2. If you could learn something through this, what would it be?
3. If God could speak to you through this, what is something he would say?
4. What are 5 reasons this breakup will be good for you?

Self-rejection
or condemnation
can be a sign
that you
don't
trust
God.

The Breakup
what to do when it happens to you

Now before we get too far ahead into the getting over it zone, let's focus on that looming moment and how to handle the actual breakup.

things you can do when someone is breaking up with you

1 **Listen to their goodbye speech**, tell them you are sorry to hear it but you understand, and then say goodbye.

2 **Tell them** that you are glad they told you their feelings and **you completely understand** that they have to go with their gut feelings.

3 If the only thing you want to say is going to be mean, then **nod** your head, turn around, and **walk** out.

4 Tell them that it has been nice getting to know them, **wish them luck**, and then turn around and leave.

5 Let them know that because of how you feel for them, you can't continue to be friends and it would be best for you to just **go your separate ways** and remember each other well.

If these responses to a major heartbreak seem very short and unemotional, it's because they are. Now listen, if you have been going out with the person for two years and there has been a lot going on between you, then you might need to talk it through. But if you haven't been together eons, then keep this breakup short and to the point. Showing emotion is okay, but breaking down and having a soon-to-be-embarrassing moment will not help you at all. And it certainly won't help them. I know that their feelings aren't your major concern right now, but think about it. You care about this person, so keep the faith, treat them how you would want to be treated, and let them have their feelings and their choices. Don't shove your emotions and your pain onto them. Get out, go home, cry into your pillow or on a friend's shoulder, go play ball, do whatever it takes to handle the pain. This relationship is over. Don't keep dragging it on.

10 Things Not to

1. **Don't ask them what you did wrong.** Anything they say here will destroy you more. So don't go there.

2. **Don't beg them to change their mind,** *because they just might.* Then you are stuck in a relationship where you are destroying each other. You won't trust that they are there because they really like you, and they won't really want to be there. Yuck!

3. **Don't argue with their decision.** It will only make you feel more rejected when they stick to it and will make the whole thing much more of a trauma.

4. **Don't yell at them.** Lashing out and trying to destroy them is not the best option. It won't make you feel better and it will make you look bad.

5. **Don't cry like a baby.** Showing emotion is okay. It's normal. But fight off the sobbing until you get out of there.

6. **Don't promise to get revenge on them.** This is a desperate try at manipulation. You are better than that.

7. **Don't remind them of all the good times you've had together.** All this will do is make you feel worse because you will be remembering all the good times that are ending.

8. **Don't tell them the list of what you think is wrong with them.** This isn't a slamfest. No matter how much you think it will help, when you leave you will still be feeling just as empty.

9. **Don't run out and tell everyone what a jerk they are.** That will only make you look bad. Handle yourself with grace, be cool, be calm, and save your breakdowns and anger for your bedroom.

10. **Don't act like they have destroyed you,** *because they haven't.* They haven't even hurt you. I know, that doesn't seem true, but the pain is there because your expectations did not match up with reality. The only way you will be destroyed is if you let yourself be destroyed. It isn't what happens to you in life but what you think about and how you react to what happens to you in life that matters.

The

pain

is there

because your

expectations

for the relationship

did not

match up

with

reality.

Why?

10 reasons they might give for breaking up with you

1 The "I just need space" breakup

This breakup is interesting. Sometimes when people break up, they say they just need some space. Half the time it is just a way of saying, "I don't want to date you anymore," but the other half of the time it means, "I feel smothered by you." If this is the case, then the best thing you can do is stop smothering them. The key thing when you are being broken up with is to realize that the best thing you can do is take their word for what it is and honor their request by backing off. If someone feels smothered, the worst thing you can do is pursue them. So back off. Take the breakup like a trooper. Don't show your pain. Don't whine to them; that only proves to them that you are smothering. Don't call them after the breakup. Don't cry to them. Don't smother them any more than you have, and you might actually prove them wrong.

Sometimes when someone says they need space, all they really do need is space. So give it to them. Their sense of your neediness might fall away, and they might return to you.

2 The "I want to date someone else" breakup

This breakup line totally kills. No one wants to hear that from the one they love. Pure agony. But the truth is that in any breakup, the bottom line is that they don't want to date you, and that means they will date others. So really, in any breakup they are wanting to date other people. You have no choice with this one. Don't try to compete with the other person or plead your case. Don't get angry with the other person; it isn't their fault. It was the choice of your boyfriend/girlfriend, and that choice was theirs to make. So lay off, lay low, and deal with your wounds in private.

Why?

3 The "It's not you, it's me" breakup

The truth is, it's *not* you, it *is* them. Their decision to break up with you has to do with what *they* want, not with who *you* are. I know you don't believe them. Your gut tells you it *is* you, but you have to fight that temptation. This breakup is about them making a choice, not your inability to be perfect.

4 The "I'm going to a different school" breakup

This is actually a very adult reason to break up. They are being honest with you and telling you that it will be hard to be away from you in a new life and not date other people. Whether you like it or not, college is a place where new experiences are around every corner, and that includes dating. So don't beg to stay with them, because it will only be worse once they tell you they've started dating someone.

5 The "I just don't want to see you anymore" breakup

I know you want to know why. You want a better reason than this. You want reasons, dates, episodes, all the details, but sometimes there isn't any one thing they can point to. They just don't want to see you anymore. They might be bored, they might just be ready for something new, but whatever it is, it isn't your right to know. So don't ask. Take it like a big person and move on. They have a right to their own thoughts and decisions.

It is pleasing to human vanity to believe that one suffers because of one's virtue; but not until a man has rid himself of every sickly, bitter, and impure thought can he be in a position to know that his sufferings are the result of his good, and not of his bad qualities. —James Allen

Why?

6 The "Something else is my focus right now" breakup

To that I say, Good! High school isn't a time to get distracted; it's a time to focus on your destiny and dreams, and sometimes a dating relationship can get in the way. If your bf/gf wants to focus on something else, let them. Support them. And you never know, in the end, they might remember how supportive you were and come back to the relationship.

7 The "I don't trust you anymore" breakup

Ouch! This isn't something you want to hear, but if you hear it, then you gotta suck it up. Trust takes time to build, and if you did something to break their trust, it will take time to get it back. And arguing about it with them won't help. Tell them you are sorry and then let them move on. That is the most gracious way to handle this one.

8 The "I caught you with someone else" breakup

Shame, shame. If you were caught with someone else, don't think that's easily forgotten or gotten over. It's the hardest thing to get over in a relationship, and you can't convince them it won't happen again. You'll just have to prove it to them. But think, if you were with someone else, then this person probably isn't the one for you anyway. Move on and put this behind you. But check yourself that this doesn't become a habit. If you think it will, then don't commit to anybody till you are ready.

9 The "I just don't love you anymore" breakup

How could they? How could someone just stop loving you? I know, it seems impossible, but the truth is that the feeling they *thought* was love doesn't feel good anymore, and so they've decided they are out of love. Learn from this: You don't want anyone who loves based on a feeling. Love is dedicated in good times and bad. If you are dating someone who only loves you when it feels good, then they don't love you.

10 The "This relationship is just too much pressure for me" breakup

That's too bad, really, because a relationship shouldn't be a pressure, it should be a pressure reliever. Maybe you put too much pressure on them to be what you wanted them to be. Try to loosen up next time. Or maybe they just put too much pressure on themselves, in which case they need to loosen up. High school is not a time for high-pressure relationships. Some people just aren't ready for the commitment, and that becomes a pressure. So let them be free. Don't pressure them more by demanding that they work it out. Too much pressure!

So there it is. Just some thoughts on what to do in the middle of the storm. Yeah, it will still be hard, it will still hurt, but you will be able to get out of it without a shattered life if you only stay in control. "Be self-controlled."

"Let's just be friends"

Breaking up does weird things to people. Sometimes after the breakup the relationship seems to get better. It's more fun. The other person becomes more attentive and even more affectionate. It will make you question if you should stay with it since it seems so good. **This is a lie!** The relationship is not better. So what's really happening here?

- Maybe they are trying to soften the blow of the breakup and they think this helps.

- Maybe they feel free to be more attentive now that the pressure of the relationship is off.

- Maybe they can't be alone and unconsciously will be super nice until they secure a relationship with someone else.

No matter why this phenomenon happens, the other person probably doesn't even know they are doing it and wouldn't admit it if they did. So this is where you have to take a stand and remember that this new relationship vibe is a lie and not the real deal. Don't sit by like a dog looking for table scraps. Let the relationship be over.

by Justin

PRIDE
ALERT:

Don't try

to get your crush

to like you again

so you can break

up with them.

That's totally not

cool, and

it won't

work

the way

you think

it will.

by Justin

You are going to feel like you've been rejected. That is part of . . . well . . . rejection. But there's a bigger picture than just losing your crush. The thing that makes all of this so badtastic is that it throws the kibosh on your dreams—all those fantasies of the future that you had built around this person are now being torn to smithereens, especially if the two of you were super close. See, it's really all the hopes you had for the future that are now crushing your heart, not the person.

You are going to have some crazy-hard times. You are not going to know what to do or where to turn. That's normal. You have become used to having the other person around, and now they're not. But this is just part of the letting go process that you have to go through. So now it's time to **take some action to get your life back on track**. It's time to get down to the getting-over-it. You feel destroyed, heartbroken, and confused. The breaker and the breakee both have some major processing to do. Don't just walk away and pretend it doesn't hurt. And don't grab on to the emotional pain and make it your life. Let's get over it.

Before you get going, you have to **take a real-pill**. You are going to have to get totally honest with yourself and with God. Remember, there's always a lot more going on than you see. It's not just about a breakup. It's about who you are and who God is. So to get started, answer these Q's. (Honestly. Hey, I don't care if you lie to me or not, but if you are going to get past this junk and get stronger in the process, you'd better answer for true.)

What is the main reason for the breakup? (If you can't think of one, take a guess. You may be right.)

Try to **put yourself in your ex's shoes** for just a minute. See them the way God sees them—forgiven. Now try to think about why they might have chosen to break up with you. Write down what you honestly think they were feeling.

Now check out 1 Corinthians 13:4–7.

Do you see the difference between romantic-type lovin' and the real kind of love we are supposed to have for other people?

Now, do you still love them?
    If yes, then how can you do that now? Your relationship is over, so
    how can love operate in this sitch?

What does love look like?
    Does it get revenge?
    Does it give space?
    Does it pray?
    If you really loved them, what would you do?

Read Luke 23:34. If Jesus could forgive people
who were torturing him to death, you can forgive your ex.

Circumstance does not make the man; it merely reveals his thoughts to himself.

—James Allen

Breakup Quiz

How well are you handling the breakup?

1. **When my gf/bf told me they wanted to break up, I:**
   a. asked them why
   b. begged them to give me a second chance
   c. told them I understood and left it at that

2. **The day after the breakup, I:**
   a. called my ex to see if they changed their mind
   b. cried all day
   c. called friends to see if they knew anything about it and could help get us back together
   d. thought of ways to get revenge

3. **Right now I:**
   a. hate them for what they did
   b. am really sad, but I have to let them go
   c. am working on ways to get them back

4. **When I think about 6 months from now, I think of:**
   a. being back with them
   b. being over this yucky feeling
   c. still being miserable without them

5. **Although it doesn't feel like it right now, I know that this will get better.** T   F

Scoring

1. a = 2, b = 3, c = 1
2. a = 3, b = 1, c = 3, d = 3
3. a = 3, b = 1, c = 3
4. a = 2, b = 1, c = 3
5. T = 1, F = 3

5–7: Keepin' It Real. It looks like reality and you might just be good friends. You seem to understand that breaking up wasn't your fault and it wasn't the other person's fault. It's just a fact of life. Sure, you hurt really, really bad, but you know that this too shall pass.

8–15: Heartache. The pain is overwhelming right now, but I promise you, it will get better. Try to remember that God wants you to look at the true and good stuff, not the bad stuff. Keep your focus on good things in your life like your faith, your family, and your friends, and don't let your brain wander off and confuse the truth with fiction.

Fear

isn't caused by approaching trials, but by

weakness

of the mind.

—Chrysostom

Trauma Treatment
getting over it

There are three major trauma levels we need to get you through before you can even see clearly enough to start getting over this breakup.

Stop the Blame Game

Being rejected by the one you love hurts tons, and "It's all *their* fault!" I know. Most people in your sitch blame one of three people: they blame their ex for hurting them, or God for allowing it happen, or even themselves for being so stupid. But let's stop that game for a minute and look at it scripturally.

Deciding not to date someone is not a sin. While it is a sin to gossip about them or try to hurt them, chances are your ex wasn't out to get you, they just didn't want to date you anymore. If you are accusing them, either consciously or subconsciously, of committing an evil act (a sin) that they didn't commit, then you are way off. And be careful not to accuse them of hurting you—that isn't the sin. Sin is disobeying God and going against his commands.

If you are convinced that your ex has sinned in your relationship and they are a believer, then you have an obligation to confront them about it. And you are scripturally bound to forgive them. News Flash: Forgiveness means you promise that you won't use this sin against them in the future, you won't talk to other people about it, and you won't dwell on it yourself. Check out Matthew 18:15–18 and Mark 11:25 for more info. And remember, forgiving might not *feel* like something you can do, but it isn't about feelings. It's about obeying God. He doesn't say you have to feel a certain way in order to forgive; just forgive, period. Don't let feelings keep you from obeying God.

Another big "beware" is blaming God for your pain. I know, "He's in control of everything, so why would he let this happen?" you cry. "Is he out to get me?" Stop that line of thinking right now. God does not cause bad things to happen to you. But he has given human beings a wonderful gift of free will, and with that comes pain. Your ex had a choice whether to leave you or not. God didn't manipulate him like a puppet on a string. God allows us to make our own decisions and then to live with the consequences. If you're blaming God, then learn more about your God (see James 1:13–18). He is loving. He cares for you, even in the midst of this trauma. And he is never, ever to blame for the bad that happens to you. But he is responsible for all the good that comes out of it. So thank him for the good he will make of this mess (check out Romans 8:28).

And finally, you could be blaming yourself for messing up, but let me offer you this: You *might* have done something wrong, but that is irrelevant because Christ's death offers complete forgiveness (1 John 1:9). If you've sinned and confessed it, walking away from doing it ever again, then you are forgiven. You aren't being faithful by holding a grudge against yourself or calling God a liar by not accepting his forgiveness. And if what you did was not a sin but just a mistake, then learn from it, dust yourself off, and move on. Again, you have no right to hold yourself guilty of what God isn't holding you guilty of.

Okay, to seal the deal, go to God with this problem and let him know that you want to be faithful. Read the following prayer and agree that this is how you want to honor God.

Heavenly Father, I am sorry that I have held a grudge against (name of person). They have not sinned against me or you, and therefore I have no right to hold anything against them. Right now I choose to forgive (name the person) from my heart for all the things he/she did to me. I promise to let them go free. They do not owe me anything; they are debt-free. I release them to your hands. Now teach me to love them in spite of how I feel. I know I can't do this on my own, so let your forgiveness and love flow through me to him/her. Now, like your Word tells me to, I pray for them to receive your blessings in the name of Jesus. Amen.

Most excellent! You might have felt a release when you did that. If you didn't, that is okay too, because faith isn't about feeling. Most of the time when I forgive people, I don't feel much of anything, but it's a command and, oddly enough, it totally changes what I think about the person and how I act toward them.

Now go back and pray that for each person you have held guilty in your heart. Remember, we are to pray for our enemies, not condemn them (Matthew 5:43–44). Get that business cleared up so we can get down to the business of moving on.

If I immediately take away the pain, then it won't bring persistence. And if persistence isn't allowed to finish its work, then you will be left immature, incomplete, and lacking a lot of cool stuff. —God

(see the book of James, chapter 1, verse 4)

I know you hurt. I know the emotions seem paralyzing, even, but if you are a person of faith, then you have to discard that crutch of hurt emotions used by the secular world—"I can't go on, I'm just too hurt!" As believers we do not live by emotions. We aren't controlled by them, because if we are, then where is God? In line *behind* our emotions? No, God makes it very clear that we are to put no gods or idols before him, not even our emotions. If your emotions cause you to refuse to obey Scripture then they are sinful, period, the end. So if your feelings are causing you to harbor resentment or hatred for someone, they are causing you to sin, and if they are telling you that you can have no joy because you are too depressed, they are causing you to sin. Guys, Scripture makes it very clear that we are to get over it:

> Consider it pure joy, my brothers, whenever you face trials of many kinds, because you know that the testing of your faith develops perseverance. Perseverance must finish its work so that you may be mature and complete, not lacking anything.
>
> James 1:2–4

Notice it doesn't say, "Mope around and feel bad whenever you face trials of many kinds." James is calling us to action—the action of getting over it. Turn your agony into joy. How? Well, first of all, by not worshiping your pain as if it were your god. You might have done that in the past, but we are called to a change, and that change is putting off your old self, getting rid of what you used to accept.

"You were taught, with regard to your former way of life, to put off your old self, which is being corrupted by its deceitful desires; **to be made new in the attitude of your minds**; and to put on the new self, created to be like God in true righteousness and holiness" (Ephesians 4:22–24).

The "putting on" part of this is changing your way of thinking. If you can begin to think biblically, trusting that God's Word is true, then you can replace those old negative thoughts with new honest and faithful thoughts. And then you will find that feelings follow action. If you can take action to learn God's truth, your feelings will soon fall in line with that truth, and you are sure to feel better, although feeling better should never be your goal as a believer—pleasing God should be the main goal. When your goal is feeling better, you end up making an idol of your feelings yet again. But when you just wanna please him, you'll never go wrong. Feelings follow actions, so change your actions and see what happens. Scripture makes it very clear:

> But the man who looks intently into the perfect law that gives freedom, and continues to do this, not forgetting what he has heard, **but doing it—he will be blessed** in what he does.
>
> James 1:25

> Now that you know these things, you will be blessed if you **do** them.
>
> John 13:17

For more help on overcoming the agony of breaking up, check out Proverbs 3:11; John 16:33; Romans 8:28; 1 Peter 1:6–7.

Trauma Level 3
Learn to Love Again

Did you know that love isn't a feeling first? Sure, one side effect of love is feeling good, but you don't *have* to feel good first to love someone. How do I know? Glad you asked. Can I command you to feel something? Like can I say, "I demand that you feel giddy right now" and make you feel giddy? Is it possible? Can feelings be ordered? Of course not! Preposterous! Everyone knows that you can't control feelings. Okay, then while you are agreeing with me, let me show you this:

Love the Lord your God with all your heart and with all your soul and with all your mind and with all your strength.

Mark 12:30

If love were a feeling, then how could God command us to love him? You might need to read that again. *If love were a feeling, then how could God command us to love him?* You getting it? Love is not a feeling first, it is a choice. You choose to love God. It's the same for him. Scripture says that God loved us while we were still his enemies (Rom. 5:10). In loving us, God proved that love isn't about feelings.

If love were a feeling, we could only obey Scripture when we felt like it. Obviously that's a crazy idea. You love because you are commanded to . . . or do you? Jesus told you to love your neighbor as yourself. Are you doing that? Neighbors aren't so hard to love, most of the time. But how about this one? *"But I tell you: Love your enemies and pray for those who persecute you"* (Matt. 5:44). That one's a little harder, and yes, it includes that "jerk" who dumped you. If you want to please God, you will choose to love those yucky people who hurt you. In fact, you really don't gain anything by loving the nice ones, the ones who love you back. *"If you love those who love you, what reward will you get? Are not even the tax collectors doing that?"* (Matt. 5:46).

See, God commands us to love, no matter how we feel.

If you wanna get through this trauma God's way, the only way, then find out what love is and choose to do it. Here's a leg up for you—the definition of love, according to our God:

Love is patient, love is kind. It does not envy, it does not boast, it is not proud. It is not rude, it is not self-seeking, it is not easily angered, it keeps no record of wrongs. Love does not delight in evil but rejoices with the truth. It always protects, always trusts, always hopes, always perseveres. Love never fails. But where there are prophecies, they will cease; where there are tongues, they will be stilled; where there is knowledge, it will pass away.

1 Corinthians 13:4–8

Find out what pleases God and do it, and your life will straighten out. The pain will end and the fun will kick back in.

Self-help books about how to survive heartache are all over the place, but I'm telling you that the only book you need is the Bible. It has all you need to get over this trauma and move on to victory. The only catch is that you have to believe it to be true and then obey it. If your goal is to love God and do what pleases him, then the obeying part comes easy. You just do it. So stop the blame game, get over it, and learn to love again.

"If you love me, you will obey what I command" (John 14:15).

Relational rehab

by Justin

Okay, emergency trauma issues should be handled. Now it's time to get you in rehab. There are lots o' ways to get over your pain, but here are a few positive tips that will help you with the transition from pain to power and from hurt to healing. Find the ones that work best for you and run with them.

Look for what you can learn: Continue to ask yourself this over and over and over, in the little stuff and the big: What pleases God in this? How can I obey his commands?

Accept that it's over. Don't skip over this one. Every time you think about your ex, just take a deep breath and say, "Nope, that's over."

Deal with the embarrassment. So much of the pain actually comes from *worrying about what other people will think*. I know this is hard to deal with, but power through it and realize that people have other stuff to consume their day besides thinking about you and your breakup. Check out Galatians 1:10.

Choose your confidants carefully. You can tell how mature a person is by how many people they tell the story of the breakup to. If they tell everyone, they have serious issues and they need to deal. That's called being a gossip. If you have more than about 3 solids you can go to, you have too many. Pick just a couple you can trust. Satan wants you to talk about the negative a lot so you can get all those negative emotions embedded in your brain. So less is more. Proverbs 16:28—check it out.

Your life in print. Journal everything. Your thoughts, your fears, everything. Make sure you jot your thoughts about what God is doing. Write the verses that he keeps putting in your head. Keep the notes flowing.

Get creative. What do you enjoy? Writing, painting, even hiking through the woods? What is something that brings you real joy? When do you really feel peaceful and connected to the Creator? Go do it.

Make a List-O-Yucks. Write out a list of all the things that you didn't like about your last relationship. The way you acted, the way they acted. The way they treated you, the way you treated them. Then you will be able to say, "Oh yeah, that's why I won't get back with them."

Forget the "if only" stuff. Yeah, there will be times when you start thinking, If *only* I had done this or that differently. Stop! Remind yourself that it's over. You don't want the relationship back. So who cares if you would have done stuff differently? When those thoughts come, stop them instantly and replace them with a verse or a thought about God. Otherwise they will come right back at ya.

Get friendly backup. Muy importante! Get your friends to fill you up with truth, God's Word, his love. In fact, set yourself up for success. Tell them exactly what you need them to say and when you need to hear it. Find the verses that support you and keep you on track, and share them with your friends. Give a verse to them on a 3x5 card and say, "Read this to me if I ever freak out."

Get a God list. This is the opposite of the List-O-Yucks. Write out all the stuff that God wants you to do in relationship to others. Pay special attention to the things you weren't doing or experiencing in the last relationship. Then read this over and over to remind yourself what God asks of you in relationship to others.

Do the exact opposite of what you would normally do. If you would normally run off and be alone "just to process everything," then force yourself to go be around people. If your norm is to jump in and find another person, then force yourself to spend some time alone. If you eat when you are depressed, don't. If you listen to music, sit in silence. Whatever you would normally do, do the opposite. This will force you to grow through the situation.

Help other people. Here is a weird life thing: If you want to feel better, help other people. Somehow God flows his healing power through the people you help. And for reals, life feels a whole lot bigger and better when it doesn't revolve around you. Wanna get over your grief? Get on with giving.

Keep their secrets. One thing you don't want to do is go off blabbin' all your ex's dirt, even if that's what they did to you. It won't make you feel better. Pretty soon you will want to take it back, but it will be too late. Your integrity will be ruined.

Forgetting what is behind and straining toward what is ahead, I press on toward the goal to win the prize for which God has called me heavenward in Christ Jesus. —the apostle Paul, Philippians 3:13–14

Say no to slam-fests. It will be hard not to bash your ex. But that would only make you look stupid, because, hey, if they were that horrible, you must have been an idiot to go out with them. "Get rid of all bitterness, rage and anger, brawling and slander, along with every form of malice" (Eph. 4:31).

Don't jump right back in. The easiest way to numb the pain is to jump back in the dating pool, but that's a bad move. It's moving your dirty baggage from one mess to another. Deal with your issues first. Take your time before you bounce back in. Healthy relationships are slow relationships.

Shove the Bible into your head. All of this rehab will boil down to fighting the battle with the Bible. Use what it says to overcome the pain. Keep reading this book and you will get a good battle plan of how to do this.

How strange it is to dishonor God by not trusting him to protect you. Why don't you be consistent in your faith? Instead of just trusting him for some things and not others, trust him and say, "I will do my part. I won't blame my circumstances or this person. And I trust that you'll do yours and take care of me." It is an act of faith to accept another's rejection rather than to fight to prove them wrong.

Breaking the
Breakup Blues:
making breakups easier to handle

All over the Bible we're told that if you can control your mind, you can control your feelings. Even researchers have proof to back up that truth. That means you don't have to be tortured by pain and agony like you might think. I know a really cool little trick that will make stuff like this breakup a lot easier to live through. But, like anything good, it takes work. So you have two choices right now, and only one is godly:

You can stay miserable and pray that someday it will just wear off by itself. 1	**You can try something new and see if your whole life doesn't do a major flip-flop.** 2

If you are up for the flip-flop challenge, here goes:

It's not what happens to you but what you think about what happens to you that affects your emotions.

It's like this: Let's say there are two people; we'll call them Solaray and Molaray. They are both in an avalanche and end up with really bad frostbite, broken bones, and horrible headaches. Solaray whines about this horrible avalanche that messed up his life. I mean, heck, he lost a toe to frostbite, what could be worse? His life is miserable, and he's totally depressed 'cuz he is toeless.

Now Molaray, who lived through the same trauma, feels way different. He's okay with life. He thinks everything happens for a reason, and so there must be something cool about this avalanche. I mean, he *did* get interviewed by every news show, including *Good Morning America*. He might even get to write a book about the whole thing. Sure, he lost a toe and broke some bones. He'll be in the hospital for at least another month. But he's whistling instead of whining. He's happy instead of sad.

So what's up with the avalanche? How come one guy says it was cool and the other guy says it sucked? Well, it sure isn't because the avalanche has all this power over people's emotions. Only people have power over their emotions; natural disasters don't control people. It's all about choices. Avalanche happens, now choices have to be made. You gonna whine about it or smile about it? You can't fix it, change it, or redo it. You can't analyze it to change the way it turned out. **You can't do anything but decide how you are going to feel about it.**

Freaky thing, but you can look at any catastrophe anywhere in the world and find two people who feel totally opposite about the whole thing. And it's all because of how they think about the situation. Change your way of thinking, and you change your way of feeling. It's that simple.

Sounds easy enough, but how are you possibly going to learn how to control your mind long enough to control your emotions? I mean, you can't even concentrate long enough to read an entire chapter of your bio book, so how can you focus your mind to beat your emotions?

Well, check this out.

It's like a DVD—your mind, that is. In your mind you keep playing these old movies over and over. Stuff from the past, stuff about that terrible night, that awful set of events. Bad stuff, good stuff, freaky stuff, stuff that makes you worry and cry and freak. Each day you choose to play this DVD over and over in your mind or to think thoughts over and over. And out of that show in your mind comes your emotions—all those feelings that you don't know where they came from.

What we are getting to now is probably going to serve you best long after the breakup. If yours is still fresh, then save this for a month or so down the road. You need some time to grieve and mourn the loss, but after some time has passed, it will be time to completely get over it. You can't live in agony forever, and you need to move on. So use this after the dust has settled.

Now the how-tos:

Okay, if the dust has settled and you are ready to forget the entire thing, here's what I want you to do. Remember that fateful day. Remember the big breakup. Now close your eyes—no, not now, after you finish reading this!—and remember the situation, how horrible you felt, how uncomfortable it was, who was in the room, and all the gory details. Okay, do it now and then read the next paragraph when you are done.

How did that feel?

Awful, huh? Breaking out in cold sweats, maybe? That's good. It's just what we needed. Now, get ready to try this: Take a deep breath, close your eyes, and think about an exhilarating moment in your life. Sometime when you were really on top, the hottest thing around. Maybe it was when you were performing for your family and they were all laughing and clapping. Or maybe it was when you got a really good grade on a test. Something that makes you feel really good. (If you can't think of a real one, make one up.) Now imagine that moment. Feel all the great emotions. Smile while you do it; it will help you feel the good parts. Seriously, it works. Okay, go.

(Don't read on if you haven't done this stuff, 'cuz the rest of this will make zero sense!)

Okay, got the good vibe flowin'? Did you feel the high? Now the fun part. We are going to replace the old video footage, or thoughts of the breakup, with this good footage. Putting off the old self and on the new one (Eph. 4:22–24).

Read all of this paragraph before you start your imagination. Here's how it will go: You're gonna start to remember the breakup.

Faith is the acceptance that

Feel it. Know it.

Then once you have those emotions down, I want you to imagine your good scenario like a movie shown on a wrecking ball that is coming straight at you. All the while the bad image is still playing in front of you. As the wrecking ball with your good memory on it gets close up to your face, it shatters the screen of the old event and replaces it with this good scene. At this point you feel all those happy emotions from that good memory. Live the moment, see the good scene. Once you've moved into the good footage really well and are feeling good, stop the movie and go back to the bad event again. Do the same thing, with the wrecking ball coming at you and shattering the bad memory, then feel the good stuff. Do this over and over till the bad event becomes almost too hard to feel bad about again. Do this 3 times every day for the next week. Soon whenever you start to think of that old event, this new happy one will get in the way. You are replacing the bad with the good. It will be like a habit. Your brain pattern is literally changed by this little exercise.

See, whatever you think about over and over becomes a permanent video in your head and affects what you do. That's why the apostle Paul is so adamant about you thinking only about

other people have a right to choose not to love you.

good stuff—read Philippians 4. The Bible is better than any psychological self-help book. God gives you all you need; you just don't know how to apply it sometimes. Now you do. Practice this thing over and over till it works. Then watch that old horrible day become less and less important. Put your breakup pain in the past.

for the **Heartbreaker**

What Do You Want?

Okay, here's the deal. A breakup is usually not a fun thing, but sometimes it has to happen. But before you get down to kicking Humpty-Dumpty off the wall, you need to have your business straight. You have to have a game plan of what you are going to do, why, and how. To do that you better answer these three Q's before you ever approach the point of no return.

1. **What do I want?**

2. **What is the best way to get that?**

3. **How will it look in the future?**

Okay, the **first** one should be pretty obvious. What you want is for the relationship to be over. Sure, you wish things were different and everything was better, but it's not. And yeah, you would like to still be friends. You would like to still have some kind of relationship with the person. That's great. *But your main goal is to end the relationship.* Don't lose sight of that.

The **second** question takes a little more thought. There are lots of ways to make the relationship end, but the best way to get what you want is to *cut it off clean* and walk away. Really, in the longer-term world, this is the easiest way to change the relationship into something you want, like a friendship, even though right now it might seem the most impossible of impossibles. (More on that stuff later.)

And **finally**, how will it look in the future? This is where lots o' lives get really messed up. Most people don't paint the picture of how the relationship looks when it ends. Get it down on paper. Write down things you will and will not do together. "We will not go to movies together. We will not go out to eat. We will go to the same study group, but we will not ride together or hang out together while we are there." This sounds brutal, but it's the only way to stay focused.

Yes, write all this stuff out. Don't just think about it. Have it on paper and take it with you for "the talk." Otherwise you might end up agreeing to try something else, and as soon as you leave you'll think, "Stupid!" So take it with you, and if you have to, take it out and look at it to remind yourself what you are going to do.

The thing you have to remember about this relationship is that how much you put into it determines how much it hurts when it ends. The depth, intensity, and length of the relationship will determine the amount of separation needed. I mean, get real, if you dated just a few days or weeks, it won't be that big of a breakup. But if you had your entire life wrapped up in this person and you guys were super-connected, then that intensity will be equaled in the intensity of the separation. It will have to be extreme and complete. So think about these important questions and get ready before you take the breakup plunge.

by Justin

LOCATION,
location, location'

Thinking about a few things first will help you get going in this process. First, since you know it's going to be a hard deal, don't have the "goodbye" talk in the middle of the Tasty Freeze or at your best bud's house in the middle of a party. Find a less public place where you can both be comfortable, 'cuz your bf/gf is gonna need time to talk about it.

You can't just say, "I've decided I just don't like you anymore—see ya!" and run out the door. To be cool you've gotta have closure. And for those of you who've never had closure and are closure-clueless, that means **take time to end it.** Tell them about your decision, take care of them as best you can, and let them talk about it a bit. This ain't gonna be easy or fun, but you've gotta give the person the benefit of the doubt and let them vent a little. It's all part of the deal.

Now let's get to the details. We'll start with the easy stuff—what *not* to do. Here we go . . .

How **NOT** to break up

Don't break up:

- in a note

- over the phone

- by telling a friend to tell your bf/gf for you

- in an IM or e-mail

- before a party

- in front of other people

- on their birthday or any other big holiday

- on national TV (à la Jerry Springer)

- by making them so mad they break up with you

- by moving and not telling them where you moved

The **Dateable Law of Inverse Sensitivity:** Girls want to talk it out, guys want **to fix it**. So girls, don't beat around the bush. And guys, don't soften the blow.

your *Choice*
is reason enough

If you're thinking that you really want to break up with your bf/gf but you aren't sure it's okay, let me just say here and now that it is. You don't really have to have a reason other than you just don't feel like dating them anymore. It's your life, your choice. But if you want to see some reasons why you should break up, check out this list:

Abuse—This one seems like a no-brainer, but for some reason it isn't. You think that it's your fault, and you wanna fix it. You think that things will get better if you just do better. But that isn't it. Abuse is never okay. Never, never, no matter what you've done, it's *never* okay. So if you are in a relationship that is abusive physically or emotionally, you are in the wrong relationship. Get out now!

Destruction—There are ways that two people can destroy each other without abuse. If you find that your spirit is weakening, your heart is breaking, and you don't know why, then maybe you are in a destructive relationship. If you can't say that this person makes you better emotionally, mentally, and spiritually, you need to think about changing the situation. Relationships should make you both better, not worse.

Lies—It's a sad truth, but after one of you has been caught in a lie, it's way hard to win back the trust of the other. That's why lies are so horrific; they tear away at the foundation of the relationship and mess it up, more times than not, permanently. If you've been lied to, I guarantee you that it will take a lot of time and effort on the other person's part to ever get you to trust them again. This isn't a healthy relationship. If you can't trust the other person, then you shouldn't be dating them, period.

Cheating—Don't give in on this one. If someone is willing to cheat on you, you can't trust them. They have destroyed that. It's just a sign of bad character. If someone is willing to tell you that you are the only one and then go out with someone behind your back, they don't have the kind of character that is worthy of you. And remember, it is your crush's fault, not the person they hooked up with.

Fights—Fights are normal. When two people spend a lot of time together, they are bound to argue, and that's okay. But if fighting is a daily occurrence, this ain't a good fit. This relationship should be the most comfortable and safe relationship you have. Fights bad, getting along good.

Boredom—Be careful with this one. Boredom is a part of life, and it might be partially your fault that you are bored. But if it's obvious that there is no hope for your boredom, then walk. Don't hang on hoping for some magical improvement. Boredom isn't a good sign for the future, so break it off while the breaking is easier than it will be later down the road.

Distance—If one of you is moving, it is only natural to start to think about a breakup. Dating over long distances is tough, and if you just aren't up for the loneliness, maybe breaking up is what you need to do.

Parental Objection—If your 'rents object to your bf/gf, it's not a good sign. As much as you hate it, they are in charge of your life as long as you live in their house and take their food and money. And besides, they are usually right about these kinds of things. (You don't have to admit that out loud though.) So if you can't make it work with the parentals, breaking up might be your only safe bet. Remember, wise people seek counsel in their lives. It's smart and healthy to get the advice of older, wiser people as you drive down the bumpy road of life. (That was the deep philosophical statement for the day.)

Even when it's totally obvious that you have to break up, it can still be really hard. People who are being abused find it really hard to leave, even though most people would think it would be most obvious and easy for them. But making the decision to hurt someone by leaving them is always difficult, no matter who they are or what the circumstances.

If you have a sense that you want out of the relationship, go with that. Don't be afraid of hurting the other person's feelings, because you aren't in control of how they will react. You are only in control of your own life. In the end, breaking it off at the first sense of trouble will be much better than letting it linger until it becomes more and more painful to break up.

Let's do a little rerun action to make sure we got the basics.

Reasons why it's okay to break up:

- You don't like being with them anymore

- They are going away to college

- Your feelings have changed

- They lied to you, cheated on you, or did something to you that you can't get over

- They have plans for the future that conflict with yours

- Your parents forbid you to see them

Suffering
is LIKE hair
color: It's
ONLY temporary.
It WILL grow OUT.

for *Girls*

Okay girls, I hate to say it, but guys are kinda slow. They need lots of explaining. And, being hunters and creatures who love a challenge, they will look for every possible angle to keep you once you decide it's over. Your rejecting them is just a harder level in the video game of life, nothing they can't conquer, they think. So for a girl breaking up with a guy, it is **crucial to not hint around about things** but be totally direct. **You hint, and he'll never get the clue.** It's like when the guy in *Dumb and Dumber* asked the girl, "So what are my chances?" and she said, "One in a million." He smiled and shouted,

"So you're telling me there's a chance!" Hey, you have to tell him point blank that you don't want to date him anymore.

Girls love to talk things out. It's just girl nature. But for guys, that doesn't work so well. They will use "the talk" as an opp to try to get you back, so it really defeats the purpose. It gives them hope, and that's so not cool. Giving them hope is like lying to them. In the long run, they will be better off if they can just move on and get over you rather than hanging on to some morbid hope that they will get you back.

Bait and Switch Warning: When a girl breaks up with a dude, the biggest in his power to get you back and let you know everything is perfect. Then he'l

Mr. Short and Sweet

Girls, realize that guys are not big feeling talkers. Even though you are the one breaking up, you may still want to talk things through with him. But he may not. He may just say, "Okay, if that's what you want," and turn around and walk. If he does this, girls, do not go after him and try to get him to talk about what he *feels* about all of this. Guys need time to go away and figure it out on their own. To drag out the "feelings talk" can be just plain selfish if he's one of these kind of guys.

Mr. Emotionless

If he just sits there emotionless, I know you are going to feel like the whole relationship was a lie. You think that if you really meant something to him, he should show some sort of emotion. Anything! If he doesn't, don't let yourself get caught in the trap of thinking he never really liked you anyway. That will destroy you. Just let him go and stick with your plan.

roblem is his pride. He has lost the game. So many times he will do everything ump you. That way he feels he won the game. So watch out for the retry.

guys' turn

Fellas, for the most part you are good guys. You want to be the hero, the guy girls dream of. And breaking up with them doesn't fit the profile. So it may seem easier to just stop calling as much. Start getting busier with school or work or whatever, and then you can just fade off into the distance. Let me just say that first, it doesn't work that way, and second, it ain't cool. You have to be a man. Hey, you were man enough to get into the relationship, be man enough to get out. Face-to-face. Suck it up, be honest, and do it.

But you need to understand this before you start: **Girls are talkers.** They think and process stuff verbally, out loud. They talk in order to think stuff through; it's weird, I know, but it's the honest to googoo truth. So they are going to have to talk it out. They are going to have to get all the stuff, all the questions, all the confusion out. That's okay. Don't take any of it as a personal attack. It's not; they are just trying to figure it all out. Remember, you've had lots of time to process the breakup. For her it's new news, a fresh wound that she is having to deal with. So don't attack back. Don't point the fault finger at her. Just listen to her and try to understand that she has to get this stuff out.

the clean break

The clean break is crucial, and holding on is failing to trust God. Don't leave little cracks of hope in the closed door, hoping God could use them to get the two of you back together again. He's God. If he wants the relationship back together, he doesn't need your help. In fact, when you try to make it better, you only mess things up. A breakup is never anything you can make better by talking more or by giving in. By its very nature, it is going to hurt, so the best thing you can do is make a clean break. "But how do I do that?" I hear you shouting. All right, calm down, here are some breakup buffet choices. You can try the quick route or the longer route. Decide based on what you know about you and your soon-to-be-ex. If you just can't bear to talk about it too much, then go for the short version, but if you know that they will really need some time to talk it through, then go for the long version. And also, check out your common sense. If you haven't been going out that long, make it short and sweet. If you've invested a lot into it, then you may need more time to get through it.

> Breaking up is like taking off a Band-Aid. Would you rather do it slow or fast?

the short
breakup

1 Get them alone (or relatively alone) somewhere where you can talk. Note: If you are afraid of the person, don't go somewhere where you will be alone. Go public and have some backup around somewhere close.

2 Be nice—no mean looks or nasty comments.

3 Keep eye contact while you are talking, but don't feel like you have to stare at them. Looking down can be a sign of respect, and that's okay. Don't stare at the floor the whole time though. Look at them as need be.

4 Get right to the point. You are there to break up, not to talk about the last game or the paper you have due next week. If you need to get out the notes you wrote about what you want and what is the best way to get it, that's cool.

5 Tell them you have really enjoyed the relationship but that things are changing for you and you don't feel like you used to.

6 Don't say, "I just want to be friends," or even, "We can still be friends." Don't give them any opening that might make them think they still have a chance.

7 Don't blame them for the breakup.

8 If they get mad, don't get mad back or feel hurt. It's just part of the process.

9 Don't talk too much. You don't have to explain all the reasons you want to break up. All they need to know is that you don't feel like dating them anymore, and that is your choice. If they ask you questions about why, you don't have to say anything except that you just don't feel the same way anymore. You don't have to give them every feeling you've had throughout coming to this decision. That's your private world, and telling them might only make them feel worse.

10 Don't let them change your mind. This is the first they have heard of the breakup, even though you've had time to process it, so they might do all they can to change your mind. If they push this, just tell them that it isn't up for argument and that you have to go.

11 Don't be afraid of silence. You may say what's on your mind and there will be dead silence. Do not fill the silence by talking and trying to explain more. Just power through the silence. Let them break it if they want to.

the long breakup

1 Get them alone (or relatively alone) somewhere where you can talk.

2 Be nice—no mean looks or nasty comments.

3 Keep eye contact while you are talking, but don't feel like you have to stare at them. Looking down can be a sign of respect, and that's okay. Don't stare at the floor the whole time though. Look at them as need be.

4 Get right to the point. You are there to break up, not to talk about the last game or the paper you have due next week. If you need to get out the notes you wrote about what you want and what is the best way to get it, that's cool.

5 Tell them you have really enjoyed the relationship but that things are changing for you and you don't feel like you used to.

6 Now shut up and let them think about it. This is news to them, and they need time to process.

7 When they try to argue with you about breaking up, just listen and let them get it out.

8 After they've said what they needed to say, tell them you understand where they are coming from, but you just aren't going to change your mind.

9 Allow them to try another angle. But stick with your decision.

10 Define the new terms of the relationship. How will you interact in the future? You should have already figured this out before you got here. Be very clear. This isn't a vote. You are telling them how it will work.

11 They will want to talk and maybe argue with you about this too. Take the time to listen to them, but stick to your guns. You have a right to decide how you conduct your life.

12 It's okay for you to show emotion too. Don't think you have to be all hard because you are the one doing the breaking. Hey, it's a tough time. So you can be upset too. Just don't give in.

13 Talk until they feel like they've talked it all out or for 1 hour, whichever comes first. There is no need to drag this on; it won't make their pain any better, and it will only make yours greater.

Say What?

The biggest prob when breaking up is figuring out what to say. Here are some ideas. Again, this isn't everything. If these don't work for you, figure out something different. These statements are clear, and they lay the responsibility on you. This is very important. They also make it clear that it is your choice and not theirs. Your soon-to-be-ex needs to know that they can't argue with you about it because it's a decision you have already made. Don't water down your decision or give them an escape clause that will only drag out this relationship that you want to end.

Some things to say when you want to break up with someone:

"I've decided that I don't want to date you anymore."

"I don't want to pursue the relationship anymore."

"This relationship doesn't feel right to me, so I have decided not to see you anymore."

"I don't see a future with us, so I'm going to stop dating you."

Say something like one of these. It's short, it's easy, it's to the point. These statements don't leave any room for them to argue. After you say your piece, they might try to argue with you, but stand firm. All you have to do is emphasize the fact that you have already made your decision and the relationship is definitely ending. There is nothing for them to argue because you aren't changing your mind.

Maybe it will make more sense if you can compare this to some things *not* to say. Check it out.

what not to say . . .

"It's not you, it's me." Nice try, but nobody ever believes this. It's human nature that when someone rejects you, you assume it's because of something you did. So this statement just sounds like a lie, even if it isn't. The important thing is that you've made a decision, and you have a right to decide what you do with your life. They can't argue with your decision about your life, so keep it to that.

"I don't think I want to see you anymore."
The statement "I don't think" is a weak one. It sounds like you aren't quite sure, and that gives the other person an angle. They'll get a glimpse of your uncertainty and they will pounce. This will lead to a series of arguments where they will try to convince you that you should think differently. Don't go there—it only makes things messy.

"I don't feel the same for you as you feel for me." How the other person feels about you isn't the issue, so don't bring it up. You can only talk about how you feel. You can't assume anybody else's feelings. That's kind of arrogant. If you say this, they will have to argue with you to prove that they don't feel more than you or that you do feel more than you say. Way off topic. Don't give them something to argue about. You want to make a clean break.

"I think we should just be friends."   You can't
just be friends. The world has changed. You both liked
each other, but now one of you doesn't. So that leaves
one person still in like with one who is totally out of it.
That spells trouble.

The "let's be friends" thing is your selfish side talking,
not your protective side. It seems like a good idea and all.
It will make everything easier, and you get to keep the
person in your life so you won't be totally lonely, right?
But it ain't nice! You may want this to happen, but it
can't happen. Not right now anyway. You have to have
separation. If you don't, it's like you are trying to tear
down a house and rebuild it at the same time. You have
to totally destroy the old before you can rebuild the new.

Plus, going from boyfriend/girlfriend to friend removes
one important word, "boy/girl." Don't take the "boy"
or the "girl" out of the person by making them your
"friend." Leave them with their pride and their manhood/
womanhood.

"I like somebody else more than you."   This
is just downright cruel. They don't need to know this. It
might make the breakup more obvious for them, but it
will also make them feel cheated on, devalued, and lied
to. You don't need to burn bridges when breaking up.
This is a person, with feelings, whom you are supposed to
protect. Don't rub their replacement in their face. Just tell
them you don't want to date them anymore, and if they

Don't burn *bridges* when breaking up.

ask why, say, "I just don't see us together in the future." They can't argue with how you feel. If at all possible, stay away from talking about other people. But if they know you well enough and you are really close, they will probably know the truth. If they front up and ask about you liking someone else, just say, "Yes, I do." Don't give them a line like "Oh, we're just friends" or "No, we're not dating." Above all, don't lie. Even if you justify it to yourself, it is a lie. And this will make the other person feel like everything you have said to them was a lie. It's not the vibe you want here.

So if they don't ask, don't go into it. If they do, be short and honest. You don't have to explain.

"Can we take some time off?" Chicken! Do you really want time off, or do you just want to get off easy? If it's the first, then you probably want time off so you can go out with other people. So just break up, already. If it's the second one, then I've got news for you: You aren't letting anybody off easy. You are only prolonging the pain. And the longer you let them hang on to hope, the more severe their pain will be and the more it will hurt you. Can you live life as the punisher? What seems like pain now will be nothing compared to what it will be like after they have hung on for weeks in the no-man's-land of a relationship void. So just tell them now that you don't want to see them. Don't candy-coat it to save their feelings, 'cuz that's not what you are doing.

"Do you think we should keep dating?" Wow, there's nothing like giving up your freedom of choice to someone else just because you aren't mature enough to say what you want. You may not be 100 percent sure, but don't ask the other person. Have your mind made up, and then tell the person that you want to break up. Don't put it off on them or play some kind of game.

"I don't want to date anyone right now." Sure, this may be what you are thinking and feeling right now. But when you break up with this person and next week feel differently and start dating someone else, you become a liar. Don't rationalize this. Just understand that if you tell a person that you don't want to go out with them because you don't want to date anyone right now, then you'd better not jump into another relationship.

"God told me to break up with you." Where in the Bible did it say that? The only time you know for sure that God has told you to get out of a relationship is when the relationship goes against his Word. Pretty basic. Don't depend on divine revelation to know what God is telling you to do. If you think you need to get out of the relationship, it's because you shouldn't have been in it in the first place. You made the choice, so don't go blaming God. It's not like he switched plans on you. Scripture never changes, and that is the plan to follow.

Avoid blaming God especially, *especially* if the person you are breaking up with is not a Christian. Don't let that be your witness. Leave them with grace, not with a bad taste about a God who told you to break their heart.

whose *fault* is it anyway?

You may think it's a lot easier to blame someone else than to take responsibility yourself, but beware. You can really get messed up if you start putting blame everywhere else but on you. Here are some ways you might blame someone else.

"God wants me to spend more time with him." Stop. Don't go there. When you bring God into it like this, you blame him for what you are choosing to do. If it is true that God said you weren't spending enough time with him, that is your fault, not God's or the other person's. People all over the world have amazing spiritual lives and are dating and even married. That is a cheap excuse for why you want to break up. So don't go there. The damage you do will be to God's reputation and your own.

"My parents told me I had to break up with you." Don't use this excuse unless it's true. Blaming your parents is the coward's way out. Own up to your own decisions—if you don't do it now, you'll be a coward the rest of your life.

"We went too far sexually and God isn't pleased."
Again, this may be true, but don't blame God for the breakup. It was your choice to go too far. What happens when you blame God is that you give the other person a really good reason to be mad at him. Do you want to ruin someone else's relationship with God by blaming him for your decision? I don't think so. So watch it on this one. Don't use God as your scapegoat.

"You aren't spiritual enough for me." The blame here is in two places. You are blaming them for not being at your level. And you are also blaming your faith, as if faith says that because someone isn't the same place as you they aren't good enough for you. That can damage the believer who is younger in their faith, so skip this line. And if they are of a different faith, then shame on you—you shouldn't have been dating them in the first place.

"My grades are just too important to me." So what happened? Weren't your grades important before when things were going well? The point here is to tell the truth. And blaming is never the real truth. You are breaking up because you don't want to date them anymore. If you did, nothing could get in your way. So be honest with them, and be honest with yourself. Don't play the blame game.

> **"You just aren't what I thought you were."**
> Ouch. There's no need to blame the other person for your decisions, even if they didn't measure up to your expectations. Keep that idea to yourself. Your job isn't to hurt the other person; it is to make the breakup as painless as possible. So just don't bring their shortcomings into it. It won't help anything.

●

"All sin is committed by our desire for good life and our fear of pain. But the things we do for a good life are lies that make us even more miserable than ever before." Augustine

●

breakup prep

Your Breakup Do List

- Give them the time they need to work through their feelings.
- Tell them some stuff about your relationship that was good.
- Tell them some stuff about themselves that is good.
- Take responsibility for the breakup ("I'm just not ready for this relationship," "I'm moving and I can't keep up this relationship," etc.).
- Spell out the rules of separation (no more movies together, no more hanging out at each other's house, etc.).
- Be firm; don't leave an open door for them to sneak back in and change your mind.

Your Breakup Don't-Do List

- Don't offer to "just be friends," ever!
- Don't get critical and blame them for the breakup.
- Don't let them guilt you into changing your mind; their feelings are their responsibility, not yours.
- No hitting below the belt—"you're just not popular enough," "your breath stinks," etc.
- Don't let them make you out to be the bad guy; you have a right to your own choices.
- Don't expect it to go easy. Be prepared for them to fight your decision, but stand your ground.

Your Breakup Escape Route

If they handle the breakup badly, remember that their emotions aren't in your control. You should do what you can to be kind and gentle, but how they react is their responsibility. Everyone has to handle their own emotions. If they start weirding out on you, just tell them that their actions are making you uncomfortable and the conversation is over. I know it sounds dorky, but now is not the time to be cool. It's time to figure out how to get out of there.

after it's
all over

recovery for your heartache →

Can we still be friends after we break up?

No. Sorry. I know that's not what you want to hear, and yes, I see you stomping up and down with clinched fists, screaming, "Yes we can, yes we can!" And I'm sad. Sad for you, 'cuz one day you will see that it just doesn't work. The trouble, my dear sassy reader, is that when you break up, generally one person does the breaking. That means one person is being broken. And because of this messed up sitch, one person always feels hurt by the other, and that doesn't just disappear and become a loving friendship. Trying to "just be friends" is the biggest lie that we tell each other. The one saying it doesn't mean it, and the one hearing it really wants to be more than friends! Take my advice and don't ever say, "Let's just be friends." It won't work.

can we *still* be friends?
and other breaking up questions that need answers

Do I have to say, "I want to break up," or can I just stop calling and avoid the person?

I can't believe you are even asking this one. Do you have to tell the person you've made a bond with that the bond is breaking? Let me see . . . uh . . . *yes!* You *have* to. There is no other way to live up to your full potential as a person of character than to care about other people's feelings even when that might be hard to do.

Aren't I good enough for them?

Yes, you are good enough, but you aren't for them. These are 2 different issues. Your goodness has nothing to do with them. You are 2 different people with 2 different lives that happened to cross. Just because this person has rejected you as their love, it doesn't mean you are defective or bad.

Can I call the person who broke up with me just to talk?

When you get dumped you totally want to find out the real reason behind it, and that's why calling to "just talk" isn't the whole truth. You wanna know, was it something you did, or said, or didn't do? What's "your" problem? Well, life isn't all about you, and it's not all about you understanding. See, if you really cared about the other person, then you could let them make their own decision and leave them alone. They decided to stop seeing you, so you really have no right to invade their life with all your questions meant only to make you feel better. And you know what else? When you call them, it only makes them dislike you more. It makes them uncomfortable, and they now associate that uncomfortable feeling with you 'cuz you are the reason they feel it. The best thing you can do when you've been dumped is to say goodbye and never call them to whine, complain, or try to fix things. That is a position of weakness and is very unflattering and selfish. So don't call "just to talk." It makes things messy, and in the end you just leave them disliking you even more.

To be human
—Alfred Adler
is to feel inferior.

Why did my ex say they loved me and then break up with me?

This happens a lot. And it's because they probably felt something at the time, but it might have been indigestion. The more you study God's Word, the more you realize that love isn't a feeling, it's an action. But this isn't a book about it love, it's a book about breaking up, so we'll save that discussion for another time. For now, don't blame them and get all bitter about them not loving you right. This only pollutes your spirit. Accept the fact that they are human. They will let you down. Then move on.

How do I get over this pain?

Have you ever bent your fingernail completely backwards so that it almost pulls off your skin? Or have you ever been hit on the nose or any other sensitive part of your body? Do you know how it hurts for a long time? Well, that's the way breaking up is. It hurts.

There is no magical formula to get over the pain, but there is something you can do to make it move along more quickly. I call it *leaning into it.* The funny thing about pain is that when you realize that it won't kill you, it can't kill you, you take away a lot of its strength. Part of your misery is that this pain feels so bad, you think you'll die. Truth is, it can't kill you. So let yourself feel hurt, let yourself grieve and cry and even bawl, but tell the pain, "You can't hurt me. You are part of healing, not part of destruction, so bring it on. I'll be done with you soon." Take the power of the pain away by accepting it for what it is, living in it for a short time, and then moving on. Don't give it special honor as if it will be your destruction; it will really be your construction if you let it make you into the person you were destined to be. Ya know why people say "no pain, no gain"? 'Cuz it's true. On the other side of this pain you will be stronger than you've ever been, more faithful than you've ever dreamed, and more attractive than you've ever imagined. See the other side. Focus on it and let the pain come. It will soon get bored and move on. Trust me.

What if my ex is now starting to call me to do stuff? Does that mean they like me again? What do I do?

Crackers! This one is tough. There are 2 possibilities here, and it will be up to you to figure out which one applies to your sitch.

One is that they were just scared when they broke up with you—too much pressure and all, so they let some pressure off with the breakup.

Now they are feeling not so trapped, so they give you a call to see if you are mad or resentful or anything. If you act hurt, they will see that there is no hope and will disappear again soon. If you act nice and friendly, but not overly friendly, they might start to think, "Hmm, maybe they aren't too clingy and I was just freakin' for no reason. I kinda miss 'em." That's one option.

The second is that they are just lonely and know that you are a willing, easy catch. You loved them so much, so of course you'll come back—that is, until some other little hottie comes along to fill the void. Sux! You don't want that. But the same thing still goes—no reason to get all huffy on the phone. They are not responsible for your emotions, so don't blame them. Be nice and friendly, but find out what is really going on. Why are they calling? What's going on in their life? How are things going? Have they been dating? You are going to have to play detective. And know this: If they have done this one before, run. It is just another round of heartache for you. There's no reason to start up something again that will just end in major pain all over again.

I wish I could give you the magic words that let you know what your ex is thinking, but then that wouldn't be life. Life is a matter of learning things by falling down and getting back up again. You win some, you lose some, but you never stop running the race and going after the big prize. So watch, listen, and pray. Make an informed decision and stick with it!

Wasting time deploring the past keeps God at a distance.

—Brennan Manning

survivor's
Manual

The battle is on, and your weapon is God's Word. Don't worry, I'm not just going to throw some verses to look up at you and hope it makes sense to you. I am going to give you a battle plan. You can change it to fit you, but here is a fab suggestion on how to get started.

Get some blank cards. They can be 3 x 5 cards, or go to an office supply store and buy those run-it-yourself business cards. Just pull them apart and you're set. You are going to write down each of these verses on a card. Choose one or two a day to read over and over and over. Keep them all with you so if something comes up and you need a certain one, you have it. Eventually they will get into your head. Your memory doesn't have to be perfect. Don't get all bummed out if you can't remember the verse number or you miss words. This is a battle you are getting into, and the important thing is moving forward. Don't sweat the stumbling.

Battle Supplies: *Your Essential Gear for the Battle*

First, do this verse. Read it and do what it says. Pray. Pray the way it says.

> Be always on the watch, and pray that you may be able to escape all that is about to happen, and that you may be able to stand before the Son of Man.
>
> **Luke 21:36**

You are going to have to go through this. That's part of the deal. But pray, right now, that you will be able to stand strong and you won't back down. Do it.

Pray that every day if you want. It's a good thing to focus on. Now let's get to fighting the battle.

> I will not let you go unless you bless me.

—Jacob to God, Genesis 32:26

> For our struggle is not against flesh and blood, but against the rulers, against the authorities, against the powers of this dark world and against the spiritual forces of evil in the heavenly realms.

Ephesians 6:12

You will have to use this one a lot. Remember that the battle you are in has very little to do with you and your ex. That is the flesh and blood. But it's a spiritual battle you're in. The enemy is going to try to keep you mad, upset, and hurt through it all. Rerun this verse a lot.

> Though we live in the world, we do not wage war as the world does. The weapons we fight with are not the weapons of the world. On the contrary, they have divine power to demolish strongholds. We demolish arguments and every pretension that sets itself up against the knowledge of God, and we take captive every thought to make it obedient to Christ.

2 Corinthians 10:3–5

There's so much good stuff here. Every time you try to fight off the rejection by talking trash or whining or whatever, remember that you don't have to fight that way. You have powerful weapons. One of them is reciting this verse. Whenever you want to argue about the breakup, or even when your mind starts playing the pity-party if-only games, recite this verse and take captive those thoughts. Stop them immediately and make your mind start to mind you and do what you tell it to do.

> But one thing I do: Forgetting what is behind and straining toward what is ahead, I press on toward the goal to win the prize for which God has called me heavenward in Christ Jesus.

Philippians 3:13–14

The relationship is in the past. Every time you think about it, read this verse to help you forget what is over with. The best way to forget something is to stop thinking about it over and over. So don't let yourself get started daydreaming. Stop the thoughts as soon as they come. Take them captive and send them away.

> No good thing does he withhold from those whose walk is blameless.

Psalm 84:11

You will have times when you think that your ex was the only person for you, but that's a lie. So read this and remember that God won't hold out on you.

> The Spirit helps us in our weakness.

Romans 8:26

When you feel totally beat down, fight with these words. The Spirit will fight for you.

> Trust in the LORD with all your heart and lean not on your own understanding; in all your ways acknowledge him, and he will make your paths straight.

Proverbs 3:5–6

When you are confused and don't understand, power through with this verse. Don't worry about understanding. Just keep looking for God, and the curvy road of this breakup will be made straight.

> "You will seek me and find me when you seek me with all your heart. I will be found by you," declares the LORD.

Jeremiah 29:13–14

You don't have to know how to find God. Just start looking for him every way you can think of. He's like a little kid playing hide-and-seek—he wants to be found by you. And he will be.

> Each one should test his own actions. Then he can take pride in himself, without comparing himself to somebody else, for each should carry his own load.

Galatians 6:4–5

This will come in way handy when you start thinking of all the "But she . . ." and "Well, he did . . ." arguments. And even more when your ex starts going out with someone else. Don't compare. You take care of your own stuff; let God deal with them. They have to carry their own load.

> Do not conform any longer to the pattern of this world, but be transformed by the renewing of your mind. Then you will be able to test and approve what God's will is—his good, pleasing and perfect will.

Romans 12:2

In a harsh sitch, you want to know what God is doing and what his will is. Here's how to know: Renew your mind. How? That is what you are doing by canceling out all the hurt and negative thoughts and replacing them with Scripture. You are renewing your mind.

> But this happened so that the work of God might be displayed.

John 9:3

Why? That is the first question we ask when something bad happens. Learn this verse. And don't miss what God might be doing here.

> Being confident of this, that he who began a good work in you will carry it on to completion.

Philippians 1:6

When you start feeling like God just ripped the good stuff away and left you, remember, he began a good thing, and he will finish it. You are just in the next stage of getting to it.

> Consider it pure joy, my brothers, whenever you are faced with trials of many kinds, because you know that the testing of your faith develops perseverance. Perseverance must finish its work so that you may be mature and complete, not lacking anything.

James 1:2–4

You want to have completeness. You want to have everything. Then you are going to have to keep going through this crap. In fact, get this verse in your brain, and every time something starts beating you down, remember this verse and smile. 'Cuz you know that if you power through it, perseverance will make you complete. I can't explain how. It's a spiritual battle issue—something God does.

> Now is your time of grief, but I will see you again and you will rejoice, and no one will take away your joy.

John 16:22

> I consider that our present sufferings are not worth comparing with the glory that will be revealed in us.

Romans 8:18

> And the God of all grace, who called you to his eternal glory in Christ, after you have suffered a little while, will himself restore you and make you strong, firm and steadfast.

1 Peter 5:10

When the grief, hurt, and self-pity start beating you down, grab these three and read them out loud. The suffering is going to pass, and if you keep going back to God, there will be a major payoff in the end.

> "For I know the plans I have for you," declares the LORD, "plans to prosper you and not to harm you, plans to give you hope and a future.
>
> **Jeremiah 29:11**

When you start thinking that your ex was perfect for you and that you wish you could get back with them, grab hold of these words. God is going to give you some way cool stuff. He sees the future, and he knows what he has for you.

> Humble yourselves, therefore, under God's mighty hand, that he may lift you up in due time. Cast all your anxiety on him because he cares for you.
>
> **1 Peter 5:6–7**

Keep going back and praying to God. He wants your focus on him through this. Every time you get upset, stop and visualize Jesus in front of you. Then throw your hurts and anxieties on him. That's what he died for—to take away that stuff.

> Lions may grow weak and hungry, but those who seek the LORD lack no good thing.
>
> **Psalm 34:10**

Learn this verse and think about it. When you think your life stinks and you want some good stuff to happen, then remember this verse. If you seek God, he is going to give you the good stuff.

> My son, if you accept my words and store up my commands within you, turning your ear to wisdom and applying your heart to understanding, and if you call out for insight and cry aloud for understanding, and look for it as for silver and search for it as for hidden treasure, then you will understand the fear of the LORD and find the knowledge of God.

Proverbs 2:1–5

You want to know how to find what God is doing and what you should do? There it is. Get to learning Scripture. Ask older, godly people about life, and listen to their wisdom. Look for understanding and you will find it. Hey, it's not easy, but that's the answer.

> Therefore be clear minded and self-controlled so that you can pray.

1 Peter 4:7

If you are having problems praying, remember this verse and check yourself. Where are your mind and thoughts running wild? Are you daydreaming about what you are missing out on? Control what you think and what you say, and you will be able to pray.

> Be strong in the Lord and in his mighty power.

Ephesians 6:10

It doesn't matter how strong you feel, because it isn't about your strength, it's about HIS. Don't forget this fact. Get over your feelings and remember that strength is about him, not you.

I know that learning all these verses and trying to find God in the bad stuff might sound like it has nothing to do with where you are right now. Or like just a bunch of churchy mumbo jumbo. But remember, this is a new battle you are fighting. This is not a battle against a breakup or an ex. It is a battle in your mind, fighting the lies that you might have believed before you read this book. Like with anything new, it will take a little while for this to make sense and for you to get into the swing of things. You don't have to understand it all. Just do it. Get focused and do it. All the truth you need is in God's Word, and all you have to do is follow it.

You did not lose out. God took something from you to prepare you for what he will give you.

"Never let God give you one point of truth which you do not instantly live up to."

Oswald Chambers

it's all over

It's all over. Whether you're the one doing the breaking up or you're the one being broken, now that it's over you are left with 2 options. You can *hang on* or *let go*.

No one can do this for you. No one can ease your pain. It's up to you. If you want to be the person God wants you to become, then you will look at this experience as a step on the path to the top of the mountain. It will be the only way that you can get from the dark valley to the top of the towering heights to bask in the sun. If you choose to get off this path of pain and head back down into darkness, you have no one to blame but yourself. But if you are a brave soul and choose to fight, to climb inch by inch up the rough terrain of pain, then I guarantee you that your God will honor you. He will show you things you've never seen before. He will give you love like you've never imagined, and he will show you his face in ways you've never dreamed.

A spiritual soul sees the pain that is coming around the bend and doesn't cower. He doesn't run and hide or return to the safety of his delusional hideaway. The spiritual soul fears nothing the world or others can throw at her. She is sensitive to the Spirit that fills the world with God's presence, and she is ready to stand up and say, "Take me, I will go!"

Breaking up is hard to do no matter what side of the split you are on. But there are ways to make it easier on yourself if you are willing to do the work. Don't give up on love when you are going through this. It takes lots of falling down before you can learn to walk. And it can take lots of lost love to find your one true love. Just look at it like this: This breakup isn't a sign that you will be alone forever; it's just a sign that you are one step closer to finding "the one."

So take your life into your hands and commit to the process. This is your refining fire; this is the stuff that will make you into who you were meant to be. If you run from it, no work will be done, but if you stand in the face of it and take it like a child of God, you will see a new life, stronger and more faithful. In the end you win. Remember that. You win!

the ext

ras

life support

Controlling Your Thoughts

Finally, brothers, whatever is true, whatever is noble, whatever is right, whatever is pure, whatever is lovely, whatever is admirable—if anything is excellent or praiseworthy—think about such things. Whatever you have learned or received or heard from me, or seen in me—put it into practice. And the God of peace will be with you.

Philippians 4:8–9

Above all else, guard your heart, for it is the wellspring of life.

Proverbs 4:23

Test me, O Lord, and try me, examine my heart and my mind; for your love is ever before me, and I walk continually in your truth.

Psalm 26:2–3

Create in me a pure heart, O God, and renew a steadfast spirit within me. Do not cast me from your presence or take your Holy Spirit from me. Restore to me the joy of your salvation and grant me a willing spirit, to sustain me. Then I will teach transgressors your ways, and sinners will turn back to you. Save me from bloodguilt, O God, the God who saves me, and my tongue will sing of your righteousness. O Lord, open my lips, and my mouth will declare your praise.

Psalm 51:10–15

As he thinks in his heart, so is he.

Proverbs 23:7 NKJV

Forgiveness? How in the World?

But if we confess our sins, he will forgive our sins, because we can trust God to do what is right. He will cleanse us from all the wrongs we have done. If we say we have not sinned, we make God a liar, and we do not accept God's teaching.

1 John 1:9 NCV

For if you forgive men their trespasses, your heavenly Father will also forgive you. But if you do not forgive men their trespasses, neither will your Father forgive your trespasses.

Matthew 6:14–15 NKJV

As for me, I look to the Lord for his help. I wait confidently for God to save me, and my God will certainly hear me. Do not gloat over me, my enemies! For though I fall, I will rise again. Though I sit in darkness, the Lord himself will be my light. I will be patient as the LORD punishes me, for I have sinned against him. But after that, he will take up my case and punish my enemies for all the evil they have done to me. The LORD will bring me out of my darkness into the light, and I will see his righteousness. Then my enemies will see that the LORD is on my side. They will be ashamed that they taunted me.

Micah 7:7–10 NLT

He who covers over an offense seeks love, but whoever repeats the matter separates close friends.

Proverbs 17:9

Help Me, God!

You saw me before I was born. Every day of my life was recorded in your book. Every moment was laid out before a single day had passed.

Psalm 139:16 NLT

For God did not give us a spirit of timidity, but a spirit of power, of love and of self-discipline.

2 Timothy 1:7

He gives power to the faint and weary, and to him who has no might He increases strength [causing it to multiply and making it to abound]. Even youths shall faint and be weary, and [selected] young men shall feebly stumble and fall exhausted; But those who wait for the LORD [who expect, look for, and hope in Him] shall change and renew their strength and power; they shall lift their wings and mount up [close to God] as eagles [mount up to the sun]; they shall run and not be weary, they shall walk and not faint or become tired.

Isaiah 40:29–31 AMP

Fear not [there is nothing to fear], for I am with you; do not look around you in terror and be dismayed, for I am your God. I will strengthen and harden you to difficulties, yes, I will help you; yes, I will hold you up and retain you with My [victorious] right hand of rightness and justice.

Isaiah 41:10 AMP

For I the LORD your God hold your right hand; I am the LORD, Who says to you, Fear not; I will help you!

Isaiah 41:13 AMP

When you go through deep waters and great trouble, I will be with you. When you go through rivers of difficulty, you will not drown! When you walk through the fire of oppression, you will not be burned up; the flames will not consume you.

Isaiah 43:2 NLT

No weapon that is formed against you shall prosper, and every tongue that shall rise against you in judgment you shall show to be in the wrong. The [peace, righteousness, security, triumph over opposition] is the heritage of the servants of the LORD.

Isaiah 54:17 AMP

Oh, the Pain!

Think of your sufferings as a weaning from the old sinful habit of always expecting to get your own way. Then you'll be able to live out your days free to pursue what God wants instead of being tyrannized by what you want.

1 Peter 4:1–2 MESSAGE

The suffering won't last forever. It won't be long before this generous God who has great plans for us in Christ . . . will have you put together and on your feet for good.

1 Peter 5:10 MESSAGE

Unless a kernel of wheat falls to the ground and dies, it remains only a single seed. But if it dies, it produces many seeds.

John 12:24

Your hearts and minds must be made completely new, and you must put on the new self, which is created in God's likeness and reveals itself in the true life that is upright and holy.

Eph 4:23–24 TEV

So be truly glad! There is wonderful joy ahead, even though it is necessary for you to endure many trials for a while. These trials are only to test your faith, to show that it is strong and pure. It is being tested as fire tests and purifies gold—and your faith is far more precious to God than mere gold. So if your faith remains strong after being tried by fiery trials, it will bring you much praise and glory and honor on the day when Jesus Christ is revealed to the whole world.

1 Peter 1:6–7 NLT

I have told you these things, so that in me you may have peace. In this world you will have trouble. But take heart! I have overcome the world.

John 16:33

We know that in all things God works for the good of those who love him, who have been called according to his purpose.

Romans 8:28

And then he told me, "My grace is enough; it's all you need. My strength comes into its own in your weakness." Once I heard that, I was glad to let it happen. I quit focusing on the handicap and began appreciating the gift. It was a case of Christ's strength moving in on my weakness. Now I take limitations in stride, and with good cheer, these limitations that cut me down to size—abuse, accidents, opposition, bad breaks. I just let Christ take over! And so the weaker I get, the stronger I become.

2 Corinthians 12:9–10 MESSAGE

Blessed is the man who perseveres under trial, because when he has stood the test, he will receive the crown of life that God has promised to those who love him.

James 1:12

Consider it pure joy, my brothers, whenever you face trials of many kinds, because you know that the testing of your faith develops perseverance. Perseverance must finish its work so that you may be mature and complete, not lacking anything.

James 1:2–4

Worry Sux!

If God is for us, who can be against us? He who did not spare his own Son, but gave him up for us all—how will he not also, along with him, graciously give us all things? Who will bring any charge against those whom God has chosen?

Romans 8:31–33

No, in all these things we are more than conquerors through him who loved us. For I am convinced that neither death nor life, neither angels nor demons, neither the present nor the future, nor any powers, neither height nor depth, nor anything else in all creation, will be able to separate us from the love of God that is in Christ Jesus our Lord.

Romans 8:37–39

Cast all your anxiety on him because he cares for you.

1 Peter 5:7

Don't listen to them; just trust me.

Mark 5:36 MESSAGE

Therefore I tell you, do not worry about your life, what you will eat or drink; or about your body, what you will wear. Is not life more important than food, and the body more important than clothes? Look at the birds of the air; they do not sow or reap or store away in barns, and yet your heavenly Father feeds them. Are you not much more valuable than they? Who of you by worrying can add a single hour to his life? And why do you worry about clothes? See how the lilies of the field grow. They do not labor or spin. Yet I tell you that not even Solomon in all his splendor was dressed like one of these.

Matthew 6:25–29

Fighting the Spiritual Battle

For we are not wrestling with flesh and blood [contending only with physical opponents], but against the despotisms, against the powers, against [the master spirits who are] the world rulers of this present darkness, against the spirit forces of wickedness in the heavenly (supernatural) sphere.

Ephesians 6:12 AMP

The weapons we fight with are not the weapons of the world. On the contrary, they have divine power to demolish strongholds. We demolish arguments and every pretension that sets itself up against the knowledge of God, and we take captive every thought to make it obedient to Christ.

2 Corinthians 10:4–5

Be careful! Watch out for attacks from the Devil, your great enemy. He prowls around like a roaring lion, looking for some victim to devour. Take a firm stand against him, and be strong in your faith. Remember that your Christian brothers and sisters all over the world are going through the same kind of suffering you are.

1 Peter 5:8–9 NLT

Resist the devil, and he will flee from you.

James 4:7

No weapon that is formed against you shall prosper, and every tongue that shall rise against you in judgment you shall show to be in the wrong. The [peace, righteousness, security, triumph over opposition] is the heritage of the servants of the LORD.

Isaiah 54:17 AMP

Bring it on! The more I get to deal with emotionally and spiritually, the more it lets me know that what God has for me will blow my mind!

what next?

Your strength in prayer often comes when you announce your intentions. Don't pray silently. Shout it out. Tell the spiritual world that you are taking a stand and not allowing yourself to be pulled under by this situation. It might take some time for you to pray this, but as time wears on, you will be able to say this to your God and really, really mean it. Read this prayer out loud in the A.M. and the P.M.

Prayer for Relief

Most holy and adored King of the universe, I totally adore you. I confess that I have let the way I feel decide the way I act for way too long. Today I want to stop it. I hate that part of me. I want my eyes to be on you, not on my feelings. So here, take all of my emotions. I give them to you. I would rather believe than doubt. I can ignore these silly fears, anger, frustration, and fatigue, and I choose to right now. I have self-control and I'm using it. I want to honor the blood of Christ that runs through my veins as a witness to your power. I confess that I don't know how to do any of this stuff, but I believe that because of my faith I can do anything as long as I've given it over to you. I know you will give me strength because I am following your truth and your words. Amen.

But the man who has doubts is condemned if he eats, because his eating is not from faith; and everything that does not come from faith is sin.

Romans 14:23

A person without self-control is as defenseless as a city with broken-down walls.

Proverbs 25:28 NLT

> You need not fear any dangers at night or sudden attacks during the day or the plagues that strike in the dark or the evils that kill in daylight. A thousand may fall dead beside you, ten thousand all around you, but you will not be harmed.
>
> **Psalm 91:5–7 TEV**

Prayer for Depression

Father, today I will honor you and let go of this junk that I've let torture me. The battle is on, and I am ready to fight. So thank you for all you've done for me. My life is awesome because of you. I'm beautiful, kind, loved, happy, healthy, and richer than many people around the world. I have food to eat and a roof over my head. Thank you for the sunshine and the clouds. Thank you for fresh air and for my bed. Thank you for never leaving me and always loving me. Thank you for your forgiveness. Thank you for my mind and my emotions. I am glad that I can feel things, even if sometimes they're bad. Thank you for giving me the ability to control my thoughts and whip my emotions. Thank you for letting me know that you have plans for me—plans to prosper me and not to harm me, plans to give me hope and a future. Thank you for being you. For being holy, righteous, and good. And most of all, thank you for your Son, who died for days like these and people like me. Thank you for adopting me as your kid and for making a home for me in heaven. Thank you for loving me. Thank you for being the God of the universe who's as close as my skin. I love you. Amen.

> Faith is being sure of what we hope for and certain of what we do not see.
>
> **Hebrews 11:1**

> "For I know the plans I have for you," declares the LORD, "plans to prosper you and not to harm you, plans to give you hope and a future."
>
> **Jeremiah 29:11**

> Cast your cares on the LORD and he will sustain you; he will never let the righteous fall.
>
> **Psalm 55:22**

> Don't worry about anything, but pray about everything. With thankful hearts offer up your prayers and requests to God. Then, because you belong to Christ Jesus, God will bless you with peace that no one can completely understand. And this peace will control the way you think and feel.
>
> **Philippians 4:6–7 CEV**

> "I have told you these things, so that in me you may have peace. In this world you will have trouble. But take heart! I have overcome the world."
>
> **John 16:33**

Letter from God

Dear Child,

You desperately want love. You think that if you could be loved, that horrible pain in your heart would go away. But you've got to remember that love is an action, not a gushy feeling. The love you really dream about is the love of movies—the kind that you only live with for two hours. But when you truly love someone, you give them the power to hurt you really badly. And more than likely they will use that power. But that doesn't mean you won't love ever again. It doesn't mean you were mistaken in your love or that love is a bad thing. It just means you now know the agony of love.

Love is the stuff that takes you to the cross. It's the stuff that cuts open your side, rips open your back, and nails you to a tree. Love isn't always the wonderful dream you imagine it is, but it is the fulfillment of my will. It is the greatest command: to love the Lord your God with all your heart, soul, mind, and strength and to love your neighbor as yourself. This is why you crave it so much. And the movies are why when you have it, you doubt it—because it's not all about feeling good.

When you desperately want love, when you want real love that will ease your heart, then the only place you can go is to me. The only arms that are big enough to wrap around you and heal you are mine. My love is the only love that won't ever hurt you. It is the only love that will never leave you, never forsake you. I never have anywhere else I have to go and I never have anything else I have to do. I am always with you and want nothing more than to share my love with you and take away the ache from your heart. Will you accept my love?

Love,

God

Why Don't You . . .

- Put on your favorite worship CD and thank God for all that he has given you.
- Find somebody else who is hurting or in need and do something for them.
- Spend some good time with your parents. Let them love on you like they're wanting to.
- Get out of the house. Go play ball, go to the mall, keep busy, do something to get that energy out of you.

Prayer for Worry

Lord, today is truth day. No more lies, even to myself. I'm not listening to the junk the enemy throws at me like "I have to be perfect," "I have to succeed and have everything go my way in order to be happy." Every time I think this stuff, I will let go of it and think about the truth instead. Like the fact that you work "all things together for good." That I should "do all things without complaining or whining." That I should only think of the good stuff, not the bad stuff. That I want to die to myself and not worry about what other people think of me. Today I'm turning my back on my pride. It's not what makes me powerful. I'd rather be wrong and let others be right than have to win. Today I will tell the truth even if it doesn't feel very good. I believe that my value is not in how well I do stuff or how good I look but just in being your kid. I won't base my happiness on what happens to me.

Today I tear out the old tape that used to play lies over and over in my head, and in its place I'm going to play the truth of Scripture. Today I trust you in everything. I find the good in everything. And I hope in all things. I know that whatever happens to me is just a tool to draw me closer to you. I know that you have "plans to prosper me and not to harm me," no matter how impossible that seems. I'm going to care more about others than myself, but I won't try to take care of everyone, because I know I have to leave that to you. I won't take everything personally. I'll slow down and find the forest in the trees. I won't think of my past as if it predicts my future. I will make decisions based on facts, not just feelings. Today I will stop telling myself lies and start telling myself the truth—and the truth is that each day is a big present from you, and every time I miss that, I miss the coolness of that fact forever. I will live life full on, just like you said. Thank you for your Word that teaches me how to live holy and honestly. Instead of me asking help in understanding your will today, I thank you for your answers that already exist in Scripture. Amen.

You won't need to worry about dangers at night or arrows during the day. And you won't fear diseases that strike in the dark or sudden disaster at noon. You will not be harmed, though thousands fall all around you.

Psalm 91:5–7 CEV

The thief's purpose is to steal and kill and destroy. My purpose is to give life in all its fullness.

John 10:10 NLT

Don't let evil people worry you or make you jealous. They will soon be gone like the flame of a lamp that burns out.

Proverbs 24:19–20 CEV

I tell you not to worry about your life. Don't worry about having something to eat, drink, or wear. Isn't life more than food or clothing? Look at the birds in the sky! They don't plant or harvest. They don't even store grain in barns. Yet your Father in heaven takes care of them. Aren't you worth more than birds? Can worry make you live longer? Why worry about clothes? Look how the wild flowers grow. They don't work hard to make their clothes. But I tell you that Solomon with all his wealth wasn't as well clothed as one of them. God gives such beauty to everything that grows in the fields, even though it is here today and thrown into a fire tomorrow. He will surely do even more for you! Why do you have such little faith? Don't worry and ask yourselves, "Will we have anything to eat? Will we have anything to drink? Will we have any clothes to wear?" Only people who don't know God are always worrying about such things. Your Father in heaven knows that you need all of these. But more than anything else, put God's work first and do what he wants. Then the other things will be yours as well. Don't worry about tomorrow. It will take care of itself. You have enough to worry about today.

Matthew 6:25–34 CEV

Don't worry. Just have faith!
Mark 5:36 CEV

Don't worry! I am Jesus. Don't be afraid.
Mark 6:50 CEV

Don't worry about anything, but pray about everything. With thankful hearts offer up your prayers and requests to God. Then, because you belong to Christ Jesus, God will bless you with peace that no one can completely understand. And this peace will control the way you think and feel.

Philippians 4:6–7 CEV

If God stopped thinking of me he would cease to exist.
—Angelus Silesius

Bible Therapy

In the middle of all your pain and agony right now, the Bible might not seem good for much, but believe me, it is. You can actually read it and it will heal your life. Help you fight battles. Give you hope for tomorrow. So check it out. To get through this hard time, you need some Word time. Don't know where to start? Can't figure out what to read? Relax. I've got the answer. Just check out this list. Read through it for the next 2 weeks. It will work wonders.

Isaiah 41	Philippians 3
Isaiah 42	2 Thessalonians 1
Psalm 43	Titus 3 and Hebrews 11
Romans 5	James 1 and 4
2 Corinthians 1 and 4	1 Peter 1
Galatians 3	2 Peter 1
Ephesians 6	1 John 4

To You from God

Dear Child,

My grace is enough. You don't have to have your pain taken away as well. Because of that pain my power holds you up, not your own. Would you rather I take it away so you can do it all in your own strength? It's a good thing that you are so weak and need me to help. If you weren't in so much pain, would you cling to me so much? Let me answer that: No. Your weakness becomes my strength because you need me to help you through. Don't hate your weakness; it's what gives you access to my strength.

Love,
God

Breakup First Aid: *the Bible*

Get into your Bible. Look all over it using whatever means you have—concordance, Bible dictionary, flippin' pages and randomly pointing at passages. Find all the promises you can on the character of God. Here are some to start you off: 1 Corinthians 1:9; 10:13; 1 Peter 1:5. Figure out who *God* says he is. You can talk to your parents or your pastor about who he is, but eventually they are going to point you to the one source that tells you the most about God: the Bible. Write all the verses down. Get all the good stuff about him. All his love for you, his grace, his forgiveness. Find out everything good about God that you can.

Now the drill goes like this: Keep this list close to you. Read it twice a day, out loud. Morning and evening are good times. Start and finish your day by reading the truth about the Father. This will help to retrain your brain. It will help you fight your urge to doubt. Then each time a little doubt comes into your mind about whatever, I want you to pull out this list. Tell the doubt to beat it, and start reading your verses. This is spiritual warfare, baby, and you are the king of it now. So what are you waiting for? Get going!

Hayley DiMarco writes cutting-edge and bestselling books including *Mean Girls: Facing Your Beauty Turned Beast, Marriable: Taking the Desperate Out of Dating, Dateable: Are You? Are They?, The Dateable Rules,* and *The Dirt on Breaking Up.* Her goal is to give practical answers for life's problems and encourage girls to form stronger spiritual lives. From traveling the world with a French theater troupe to working for a little shoe company called Nike, Hayley has seen a lot of life and decided to make a difference in her world. Hayley is Chief Creative Officer and founder of Hungry Planet, an independent publishing imprint and communications company that feeds the world's appetite for truth. Hungry Planet helps organizations understand and reach the multitasking mind-set, while Hungry Planet books tackle life's everyday issues with a distinctly modern spiritual voice.

As you can see by the evidence in your hands, Justin writes some really cool books. But his first love is being face-to-face speaking to groups. He has done everything from small group interactions to huge music festivals to throwing down at an event at the House of Blues. He has done nearly 3,500 programs to about half a million people. He would love to come speak at your event. And his wife is always willing to send him out of the house. He is perfect for school programs, conferences, retreats, parenting conferences, staff development, and all kinds of leadership and special events. Check out what Justin can do for you at www.lookadoo.com or email him and Emily directly at speakers@lookadoo.com. But definitely check out the website.